Dedication

This is dedicated to my Giovanni and my Guinevere. It was not love at first sight when you were cut from my uterus. I felt a pure primal animalistic need to provide, protect, and nurture you. You two are the greatest things I have ever made. And, You will always be the things I am most proud of.

Also, shout out to my brother, Sea, for coming through last minute and helping me to get this published. You da bomb!

Pre-Baby:

First off, I love love love my children. They are literally humans I 3-D printed from my uterus. They are the pieces of me that live outside my body. Just the thought of any harm coming to them (emotionally or physically) sends me into a deep dark tunnel of becoming a self-destructing bomb that not only blows myself into a million pieces but also burns the entire world to ash. I'm already anxious about the possibility of bullying and my kids are just in preschool! Those little munchkins are my favorite things, and I can't help but constantly worry about them or that I'm not doing enough for them.

HOWEVER, had I known what it was really like (I mean really really like), I'm not so sure I would have had two. That being said, there are a few things to review before you even consider having one:

1. Can you financially provide for yourself and another human being? This is huge! Just because you're expecting, does not mean money is going to begin to rain down from the heavens to compensate for whatever dollar amount you are lacking. In other words: Have your bank account looking correct. You don't need to be a millionaire, but you do need to be realistic.

2. Are you emotionally and mentally prepared for a kid? This means you need to dig deep and get really real with yourself. If you have any mental health situation from your past or present, then you need to be aware of how that can affect your future. This may mean having a consistent therapy session, talking to your doctor about medications that you can safely take and making plans moving forward on how to take the next best steps. Make sure you are doing right by your future offspring and you. This child will affect your physical and mental capacity, so it is your responsibility to ensure their home and caregiver (YOU) are providing them the safest environment to grow mentally and physically healthy.

3. Find your ducking Village (and then have a back up village in case the first one burns down). Village is just another word for support, support, support, support. Your village can consist of your partner, a sister, brother, mom, dad, cousin, friend, teacher, nanny, etc. It's anyone you can count on to help and assist you as you raise this child (or children). They will help babysit, stay on the phone while you cry at 4 am because you haven't slept in 4 weeks, cook your dinner for the first week with your infant, help drive you to the doctors when your car breaks down, buy groceries, organize holidays, and so on. These are the people that will be there to help build a nurturing environment for your little one. You are going to need help, so please please please please find a good village. The help isn't just for you, it's for your munchkin. You can't be a good parent if you're trying to juggle everything and end up burning out leaving nothing left to give your baby. Find your village (or two) and get the help. Asking for help is not a weakness. It's a boss move called delegating (but remember to say please because everyone knows please is the magic word. Duh. plus thank you is nice too.)

*keep in mind, no one is obligated to help you just because you have a kid. If you ask for assistance and the person doesn't want to help, then look for help somewhere else and fire that person from your Village.

4. Check your relationship (If you're in one). Make sure things are healthy with whoever you want to

have a child with or decide if it's best you have a child on your own or not at all. Understand the responsibilities that will be coming and what roles each of you will need to play. You and your relationship are the foundation that everything is built on. If you have cracks, then the house will fall apart and everyone will suffer (baby, cradle and all).

Decision made:

Adoption - I do not have experience with the process but I do know from others that it can be emotionally and mentally trying. Be prepared for what it will take and the finances involved. Definitely talk to others about their adoption story and the steps they went through.

Pregnancy - Be prepared for a not-so dreamy pregnancy. Yes, it's amazing what the body can do. Yes, it's magical how a human can create another. However, not all pregnancies are created equal. Both my pregnancies FELT like hell. I was nauseous and vomiting every single day for months and months and months. I hated food and water, I was dehydrated and had to take dissolvable medicine to help ease my symptoms just enough to survive. I felt like my body had turned on me and I had no control. I have never felt so weak and powerful at the same time. I was building something miraculous inside of me and losing my mind trying to force myself to eat and drink. It was even rougher the second time when I had to take care of my, then, 2-year-old. I felt inept as a mother, barely able to care of myself, let alone my toddler. I cried and had doubts but somehow managed to get through (especially with help from my family and Ms. Liza). Without my village, I would have drowned, and my first munchkin would have sunk holding on to me. So moral of the story, consider how your life will change before having a child, create a strong village, and make sure your relationship with your partner (if you have one) is strong like Vibranium.

Miscarriages are sometimes a part of the pregnancy journey. They can happen at any moment after conception. They can happen for a multitude of reasons. They can happen after you've already had kids. They can happen in a boat, on a goat, or in a float. The point is, They happen. You can do your best to avoid them but for whatever reason, a miscarriage can still take place. Many have experienced them and we don't always talk about it as much as we should. They can be difficult to process and overcome. Again, lean on your village and partner. Remember, your feelings are valid.

*Also, have a baby shower but only ask for basic-bare essentials and really push cash and gift cards. Most of the stuff you ask for will not be used because you forgot you had it, you realize it was stupid or doesn't work for your baby so you want to return it but can't because you opened it after the baby was born which is definitely more than a 30-day window to return it. With cash and gift cards, you can save it till after the baby is born and then just buy/order all the crap that might actually work for your kid and if it doesn't, you can immediately return it!

I am so pissed about the stroller I got from my registry with my first kid. I was so excited for this stroller and, I kid you not, I never used it. We opened it once and I was like 'funk this'. I sold it on an app and my mom got me something a lot more my speed.

And before you even make the registry: go to the baby stores and try everything and I mean everything! Ask an associate to open boxes, bring a doll and push it in a stroller, put a stuffed animal in a car seat, touch a blanket, practice putting a doll in a crib, sit in every ducking rocking chair you can, etc.

After Baby:

Remember to find time for you, again… ask for help (this is where the support system comes into play). If you are doing things solo, call in your village and reinforcements! Even if you have a partner, call on your village for a ten-minute shower, or a chance to mind numb with a reality show, or to bring take out cause you're tired of forgetting to eat, etc. If you have a partner, make a game plan on who does what when and where. Trade off break times, take turns taking breaks, and call your village. Everyone needs help!

*Triggers (at least for me...)
Breastfeeding - This was a tough situation for me. I had trouble producing milk and I did not take it well. I had this fantasy that once my baby was born, I would have this abundance of supply and fill up a freezer. That is not what occurred. Instead, I did not truly understand how to really get the job done. Like, there's a special technique to get the nipple in the baby's mouth and pumping or feeding every 2-3 hours (even overnight) to stimulate milk production. Silly me, I would sleep when the baby slept and didn't pump overnight. After I realized how much I didn't know, I gave everything I had to try to do it right. I pumped every 2-3 hours (even overnight), I ate milk cookies, drank teas, pumped in the shower, and got multiple pumps that I thought would help. It still wasn't enough to provide for my baby solely on my own. We had to supplement with formula. It hurt my pride, but my kid's health was more important than my feelings of defeat. My little one was born premature, and it was paramount that they gain as much weight as possible. So, for 4 months I slept 1-2 hours at a time trying to give them as much as I possibly could before I decided to completely switch to formula. I was getting worn down and I needed to let go so I could get more rest. I gave myself grace. I had to realize for myself that there is nothing wrong with formula and what's most important is the baby's health. I envy those that have all the supply to feel a

freezer, but I also respect the decision to use formula. There is nothing wrong with how you provide for your kids as long as you provide.

Sleep Training - Sleep Sleep Sleep Sleep Sleep. Everybody wants and needs sleep. Sometimes this means using different methods to help babies sleep longer at night. One in particular is the crying out method (which can get a bit controversial). I, myself, knew I couldn't handle that. Any time my infant cried; I went to them. Now, as they got older, I would introduce different soothing mechanisms to help them. As a newborn, it was changing, feeding, and then rocking with a pacifier. Months old was still the same thing but I would wait a few minutes after initial whining to see if they would go back to sleep. If the whining got louder or turned to crying, I would go to them; but if they went back to sleep, I would sigh in relief. By toddler stage they were sleeping throughout the night. Of course, there was the sleep regression with my oldest when my youngest was born. Every time the baby cried or woke up, they woke up. I thought I was going to die! Then by some miracle, I was able to get them both sleeping through the night (with the exception of being sick, scared, wet bed, etc. - The usual hell)

Potty Training - When to start, when not to start? That is the question. Some believe you need to wait till the child tells you they are ready. For example, when the child is old enough to wonder about the potty and wants to imitate you. This can start early or take up until 4 years old. Some like to try a thing referred to as elimination communication. It's basically introducing the idea of not peeing and pooping in your pants as early as you want. I, personally, did this with both my kids and both used a squatty potty early on. Before they could even walk, I would take them periodically throughout the day to the restroom, hold them over the sink/toilet and make sounds to promote them to pee or poop. It actually worked (for us)!Plus, I saved so much money on diapers and pull-ups!!!!

Find your rhythm:

I don't mean carve out a routine set in stone or blood. I mean get into your flow. If you like to have a set time when things occur because it keeps you organized and fills you with a sense of calm, then do it. If you and your family like to move in a more relaxed way where nothing is scheduled and you wake up when your eyes want to open, then so be it. You may even notice your kids formulate their own schedules. Every kid is different, and their little bodies just seem to find a pattern on their own. Find the 'rhythm' for your family and lean into it. You will have such a peace of mind when you get in your zone.

Not gonna lie, I can be a bit anal, so I feel most calm when we are on point with our schedule and I'm knocking things off my checklist. I love lists, schedules and post-it notes. I literally make an Itinerary for trips and vacations (keep in mind, I do not make everyone stick to it completely - it's more of a suggested guideline). But you should never take me to an office supply store. It's my kryptonite (as is the other store that shall not be named - you know which one).

Sex/intimacy:

Get back on that saddle, or dick or finger or whatever else is going to get those 'rocks off'! You are a parent but also a person! You still have to get back to you and one of those things is intimacy or sex. Remember your body is more than an unconditional love machine or milk machine or nap station, etc. You are still a person with desires and needs. You deserve to be touched and to feel attractive (whether by a partner or yourself). Also, being physical is good for your relationship too (with yourself or partner).

I have a problem with initiating so I made a deal with my husband that if he asks, he shall receive (and so do I). It works for us and everyone is happy. He doesn't have to play the guessing game to see if I'm in the mood and neither do I. Again, This is something we do and works for us. Find what works for you. For example, schedule it in your week and make sure it's in your calendars or send each other sexy time invites. "See you tonight at Dick'o'clock"; "Wanna cum at my pussy party tonight?"

*FYI: The first time having sex after my c-sections hurt like hell! My mound was swollen and enlarged. It hurt to pee, sit, and breathe. I had pain killers for about two weeks before they cut me off so I wouldn't become addicted. However, 6 weeks later, I was still pretty damn tender. Then,I had sex and was like holy hell, that hurts! Eventually, the pain became non-existent and sex was much better when everything healed. But, homie, that first time, was like 'OUCH'...just so you know…

The Guilt and Worry:

It's there and will always be there. You have to find a way to handle it and manage it. Do not let it overwhelm you or completely send you into a downward spiral. Get a friend, Get a therapist, keep a journal, have an ongoing weekly/monthly day or night out to decompress and unload, etc. Do whatever it takes to calm the negative thoughts and anxiety so you can be present. You must prepare yourself with the tools needed to combat these ideas.

I personally started feeling guilt and worry the moment I was pregnant with my first child. I wondered things like: Am I eating enough? too much? Is my home prepared? Can we provide properly for a baby? How will I know what to do?

Then when they were born, it was: Am I stimulating them enough? Too much? Are they reaching their milestones? Am I giving them enough attention? Do I read enough to them? Do I take them out enough? Will other kids like them? Will they make friends? Will they be bullied? Are they too hot? Too cold? Am I getting them the best foods to eat? do they know I love them? ....and on and on and on and on and on...

When my worries and guilt begin to ramble, I have to quiet my brain and remember to enjoy my time with them. I Look at their little faces that I made and take memory snapshots of our precious moments together. They are my everything and there is absolutely nobody else's vomit I would clean up from their room at 3:30 am after staying up till 12 am just to put them to sleep. Just saying.

So are you.....

Having Kids	Not Having Kids
Do not let others pressure you into this. It will get hard, really really hard. Nobody said it was easy (and if they did, they're lying cunts!) It is your responsibility to find the help, tools, inner strength, etc to pull through. That's why it's so important to make sure you are prepared. Having kids does not entitle you to anything. You don't deserve special treatment and you shouldn't expect rewards for being a parent. If you choose to have a kid, then have it because that's what YOU want. Don't have it for attention, or to save a failing relationship or because you want to guilt trip your kids into taking care of you when you're old. Your kids don't choose to be here and they didn't choose you. So, the least you can do is to give them everything you got and don't take them for granted.	If you decide not to have kids, then don't let anyone push you into it. There is nothing wrong with NOT wanting kids. You do not have to have kids to complete your life. Be real with yourself and your partner (if you have one) about how you feel. Don't let others make you feel guilty for living a life for you. Enjoy the life you want to live.

So, The publishing company I used to publish this book requires the book to be at least 18 pages. Therefore, I have added randomness...Enjoy!

I had two cesareans. It was planned and kind of unplanned. With my first, I was very adamant that I wanted to elect to have a c-section. My Ob-gyn at the time supported my decision but was definitely more team vaginal birth. However, I stuck to my guns. Mostly because I had heard actual accounts of vaginal tearing, searing pain, and possibly going through hours of labor to end up with a c-section anyways. That's basically giving birth twice for the same baby! Nonetheless, I had complications with both my pregnancies and both babies were born early. Therefore, my c-sections were planned but the due date was a bit earlier than expected.

Cover Illustrator: Julia Cubiz

Inside Illustrations by Sian Shirley, visit her darker artworks at http://instagram.com/oddiothief

Beep bop boo. Take me to your leader, BAAAAAAA!

(That's my impression of an Alien)

THE END

www.ingramcontent.com/pod-product-compliance
Lightning Source LLC
Chambersburg PA
CBHW050022040726
47599CB00014B/1501